MW01290734

MINDFUL
MANIFESTATION

*A Uniquely Effective Way
to Practice Mindfulness*

By Neville Goddard and Tim Grimes

Part of the
NEVILLE EXPLAINS THE BIBLE
Series

Personal Message from Tim Grimes

Hello! Feel free to reach out to me with questions about the material in this guide, and anything else I may be able to help you with. I also invite you to join my mailing list so you can get information on future books and events. To get in touch visit: www.radicalcounselor.com

Bulk Purchases and Speaking

For more information on discounts for bulk purchases, or to invite Tim to speak at your next event, email radicalcounselor@gmail.com

ISBN-13: 978-1516902590
ISBN-10: 1516902599

Printed in the United States of America

Neville Goddard (1905–1972) was one of the great spiritual teachers of the 20th century. He leaves a legacy of undervalued work, some of the finest which is presented and explored by Tim Grimes in this series.

Other books in the series include:

CONTENTS

What is mindfulness, really?

Honestly, I don't know the answer to that question. And I doubt you do, either.

When Jon Kabat-Zinn introduced the term "mindfulness" to the general public a few decades ago, he was attempting to incorporate Buddhist meditation practices with modern medical psychology and medicine. Kabat-Zinn's ideas were intriguing and effective, especially given the rather conservative setting in which he was applying his advice.

But we're a long way from *Full Catastrophe Living*. And the mindfulness movement is far removed from Kabat-Zinn's original ideas on the subject. Frankly, when most people use the term "mindfulness" today, it means next to nothing. Mindfulness, in modern culture, just implies some sort of open, nonjudgmental awareness. It's still usually thought to be a meditative exercise, but not always. Regardless, most people who are interested in mindfulness would probably agree that meditating, and mindfully watching your thoughts floating by without passing judgment, sounds like a lovely concept.

And, indeed, meditating in such a way *is* lovely – if our thoughts are lovely. However, if our thoughts aren't lovely, meditating on what's floating by isn't exactly pleasant. Nor is it effective – although we often fool ourselves into thinking it is. We often believe we're reducing stress by watching our unpleasant thoughts float by and not interfering with them – but, in reality, a lot of the time we're just subtly making ourselves anxious.

Here's the unglamorous truth about the mindfulness movement that most of us don't want to acknowledge: if we objectively watch our thoughts – and don't emotionally intercede with them – we'll probably observe ourselves having the same cycles of good thoughts and bad thoughts, repeating themselves again and again. If we meditate in such a way – without attempting to refine our thoughts, and instead simply letting them "be" – we'll often notice the same emotional cycles of our thinking recurring over the course of many months, and sometimes even years. Objective, nonjudgmental meditation makes us quite aware of this. Our specific thoughts will change – but we'll still usually have the same up and down emotional cycles within our thinking, regardless of the specific thoughts.

If this sounds somewhat unappealing, boring and unproductive…that's be-cause it usually is. I spent over a decade of my life meditating in such a way, and even once spent a year living at a Buddhist center to focus on meditation intensively. I put a lot of time into trying to be mindful.

And all this effort did not make me any more mindful.

This happens to a lot of people who try to practice mindfulness over a long period of time, although we're usually reluctant to admit as much. It's not easy for us to admit we're basically wasting our time. It took me many years to come to that hard, rather embarrassing conclusion – a conclusion that seems obvious in retrospect. For me, the same dissatisfying cycles of emotional energy and thoughts continued over and over again as I sat there meditating. *For years.* Still, for vague reasons, I plugged along. There were innumerable times meditating when my thoughts were very content and peaceful. There also were innumerable times when my thoughts were anxious and stress-inducing. I usually noticed all these emotional variations in my thinking from a somewhat removed mental standpoint – you could call it a mindful standpoint – and these same repetitive cycles continued on and on and on…

Now, I'm not necessarily saying anything bad about meditation, or even practicing mindfulness in such a way.

But I am saying that if you expect to *get* anything from it, you're definitely choosing the wrong path. As the wonderful Zen monk Kodo Sawaki pointedly said, *"Meditation is about loss."*

Is learning about loss why you're practicing being mindful? I suspect it's not. And if it isn't, then it's worthwhile to ask yourself, "Why am I *really* interested in this practice of mindfulness?" You won't gain anything from meditation if you practice mindfulness in the way described above. It won't make you happier. If you want to learn about the repetitive inner cycles of your thoughts and emotions, then meditating can be a good way to explore this. Some of you will be interested in finding out about this humble method of inner self-exploration.

But most of you won't.

Most of us are sick of loss, and losing. I know I am. We want to actually win sometimes. We've experienced enough loss already. We're totally disinterested in it; we've had enough lessons in losing already in life, thank you very much. Most of us meditators are so used to getting less, and we're quietly desperate to find out a way to get *more* in our life instead – even if we say we aren't. It's not that we're greedy; the problem actually might be that we're suffering by pretending to be too humble. We mistakenly think that's what Buddhism and mindfulness is all about – mindfully living through suffering. So we inadvertently suffer some more, and make it even tougher on ourselves. This happens in part because we have trouble admitting what we actually *want* in life.

But we shouldn't feel defeated and dissolute like this. And we can't just sit there and expect for anything to change after all this time when nothing's changed. It won't. We need a new approach. So I suggest we think about what we really want in life. Once we start having an idea about what we actually want in life then we can start finding it within ourselves. This is the kind of approach to mindfulness I can fully endorse. Decide what you would like in your life, and then start to feel it within yourself. This might sound confusing, but bear with me. Everything will soon get clearer. First remember this: mindfulness shouldn't be about loss; it should be about gain.

The purpose of mindfulness should be to attain what you desire. Otherwise you're just wasting your time.

There shouldn't be anything too esoteric or vague about it. We need to be practical. What would make us feel better? Having more money? Feeling healthier? Getting a big job promotion? Having a better relationship with our family? What do you really *want?*

That is a practical question worth answering. And the answer is what you should be mindful about. What do I mean by this? Well, if we want more money, for instance, then we need to become more mindful about money. This doesn't mean thinking more about money, as there's nothing mindful about that. People anxiously think about money – or their health, or their relationships, or the fancy car they want – all the time, and get nowhere productive because of it.

What I mean by being mindful is that you have to *emotionally already feel wealthier than you actually are* if you wish to become wealthier. Likewise, if you want to be healthier then you have to *already feel healthier* than you currently are in physical reality. If you want a new job then you have to emotionally feel *you already have that job*. If you want better relationships you have to feel *you already have those relationships*. If you want a new fancy car *you have to feel you already have that car*.

This is *real* mindfulness. It's not spiritual mumbo-jumbo wrapped in a pretty Buddha blanket. It's consciously focusing on how you feel, and gently molding your inner feelings to your liking. *This will, in turn, naturally and miraculously shape your outer reality to your liking.* We can do this simply by feeling relaxed and believing that we already possess what we desire.

So we're talking about something here that's a very different practice of mindfulness than what we're used to, and also one that is far more rewarding. The purposes aren't vague at all. There's a specific goal we wish to achieve, and we are peacefully focused upon it. Even a purely mental goal – like "being more in the moment" or "being happy" – has *specific* physical characteristics and feelings we can calmly latch on to and emotionally focus upon if we want to manifest such a state consistently in our lives. "Being happy" isn't a vague goal if we can consciously identify what it *feels* like to us. Material goals can be *feelings* you have successfully identified within yourself and then decided to calmly cultivate inwardly.

We practice mindfulness most effectively by feeling we already possess what we desire.

Our thoughts, in and of themselves,

don't matter much. It's our feelings that count. Whatever we feel on a consistent basis becomes part of our life. What we think about constantly, what we imagine constantly, we usually end up *assuming and feeling as being real.* Our assumptions and feelings are directly intertwined with how we live our life. So we should start being more mindful of our assumptions and feelings, and how we react emotionally to certain thoughts. If we do this, things in our life can positively transform at a shocking speed.

Here's the good news: it's not too hard to practice this type of mindfulness, *because it's enjoyable to imagine feeling what you deeply desire as already being real, to assume your deepest desires as being real.* We can gently learn to become more self-aware of our feelings and thoughts, and then gently work on modifying them to fit our liking.

This is the path of mindfulness that's far less traveled than the standard, wayward "meditation" route. And, for the majority of you, it'll be a hundred times more effective in *actually* changing your life. To further clarify this point, let's turn to one of last century's most unique and articulate proponents of this practice, Neville Goddard.

Talking to oneself is a habit everyone indulges in. We could no more stop talking to ourselves than we could stop eating and drinking. All that we can do is control the nature and the direction of our inner conversations. Most of us are totally unaware of the fact that our inner conversations are the causes of the circumstances of our life.

We're told, *"As a man thinketh in his heart, so is he."* But do we know that man's thinking follows the tracks laid down in his own inner conversations?

To turn the tracks to which he's tied towards the direction he wants to go he must put off his former conversation – which is called the *"Old Man"* in the Bible – and be renewed in the spirit of his mind. Speech is the image of mind. Therefore, to change his mind, he must first change his speech. By "speech" is meant those mental conversations we carry on with ourselves. The world is a magic circle of infinite possible mental transformations, for there are an infinite number of possible mental conversations. When man discovers the creative power of inner talking, he'll realize his function, and his mission in life. Then he can act with purpose.

Without such knowledge, he acts unconsciously. Everything is a manifestation of the mental conversations that go on in us without our being aware of them. But as civilized beings, we must become aware of them and act with a purpose.

Your mental conversations attract your life. As long as there's no change in your inner talking, your personal history remains the same. To attempt to change the world before we change our inner talking is to struggle against the very nature of things. We can go round and round in the same circle of disappointments and misfortunes, not seeing them as caused by our own negative inner talking, but as caused by others.

This may seem farfetched, but it's a subject that lends itself to research and experiment. The formula a chemist illustrates isn't more certainly provable than the formula of this science – by which our words are clothed in objective reality.

One day a woman told me of her difficulties working with her employer. She was convinced that he unjustly criticized and rejected her very best efforts. Upon hearing her story, I explained that if she thought him unfair, it was a sure sign that she herself was in need of a new conversation piece. There was no doubt that she was mentally arguing with her employer – for others only echo that which we whisper to them in secret. She confessed to me that she argued mentally with him all day long. And, realizing what she'd been doing, she agreed to change the inner conversations she had with her employer. So she imagined that he'd congratulated her on her fine work, and that, in turn, she'd thanked him for his praise and kindness.

To her great delight, this woman soon discovered that her own attitude was the cause of all that befell her. The behavior of her employer reversed itself. It echoed, as it had always done, her mental conversations with him. I rarely see a person alone without wondering, "To what conversation piece are they tied? On what mysterious track are they walking?"

We must begin to take life consciously. For the solution to all problems lies just in this: the *"Second Man"* – the Lord from heaven in all of us – is trying to become self-conscious in the body, that he may be about his Father's business. What are his labors? To imitate his Father – to become master of the Word, master of his inner talking – that he may mold this world of ours into a likeness with the Kingdom of Love.

The prophet said, *"Be ye imitators of God as dear children."*

How would I imitate God? Well, we're told that God calls things that

aren't seen as though they were seen –
and the unseen becomes seen. This is the
way the woman called forth praise and
kindness from her employer. She carried
on an imaginary conversation with her
employer based on the premise that he'd
praised her work, and he did.

Our inner conversations represent, in
various ways, the world we live in. Our
individual worlds are self-revelations of
our own inner speech. We're told that
every idle word that men shall speak
they shall give account thereof: *"For
by your words you shall be justified, and by
your words you shall be condemned."*

We abandon ourselves to negative
inner-talking, yet expect to retain
command of life. Our present mental
conversations don't recede into the past
as man believes. They advance into the
future to confront us as wasted or
invested words: *"My word,"* said the
prophet, *"shall not return unto me void,
but it shall accomplish that which I please,
and it shall prosper in all the things whereto
I sent it."*

How would I send my Word to help a friend? I'd imagine that I'm hearing his voice, that he's physically present, and that my hand is on his shoulder. I'd then congratulate him on his good fortune, tell him that I've never seen him look better. I'd listen as though I heard him. I'd imagine that he's telling me he's never felt better, he's never been happier. And I'd know that in this loving, knowing communion with another – a communion populous with loving thoughts and feelings – my word was sent, and it shall not return unto me void, but it shall prosper in the thing whereto I sent it.

"Now is the accepted time, now is the day of salvation." It's only what is done now that counts, even though its effects may not be visible until tomorrow. We call, not out loud, but by an inner effort of intense attention. To listen attentively, as though you heard, is to create.

The events and relationships of life are your Word made visible. Most of us rob others of their willingness and their ability to be kind and generous by our fixed attitudes towards them. Our attitudes unfold within us in the form of mental conversations. Inner talking from premises of fulfilled desire is the way to consciously create circumstances. Our inner conversations are perpetually out-pictured all around us in happenings. Therefore, what we desire to see and hear without, we must see and hear within. For the whole manifested world goes to show us what use we've made of the Word.

If you practice this art of controlled inner speaking you'll know what a thrill it is to be able to say, *"And now I have told you before it come to pass, that when it is come to pass, ye might believe."* You'll be able to consciously use your imagination to transform and channel the immense creative energies of your inner speech from the mental, emotional level to the physical level. And I don't know what limits, if any, there are to such a process.

What is your aim? Does your inner

talking match it? It must, you know, if you would realize your aim. For the prophet asked, *"Can two walk together except they be agreed?"* And of course the answer is, *"No, they cannot."*

The two who must agree are your inner conversation and the state desired. That is: *what you desire to see and hear without, you must see and hear within.*

Every stage of our progress is made by the conscious exercise of our imagination matching our inner speech to our fulfilled desire. As we control our inner talking, matching it to our fulfilled desires, we can lay aside all other processes. Then we simply act by using clear imagination and intention: *we imagine the wish fulfilled and carry on mental conversations from that premise.*

The right inner speech is the speech that would be yours were you to realize your ideal. In other words, it's the speech of fulfilled desire. You'll understand how wise the ancient was when he told us in the Hermetica, *"There are two gifts which God has bestowed upon man alone and on no other mortal creature. These two are Mind and Speech, and the gift of Mind and Speech is equivalent to that of immortality. If a man uses these two gifts rightly, he will differ in nothing from the Immortals. And when he quits his body, Mind and Speech will be his guides, and by them he will be brought into the troop of the gods and the souls that have attained to bliss."*

With the gift of Mind and Speech you create the conditions and circumstances of life: *"In the beginning was the Word, and the Word was with God, and the Word was God."*

The Word, said Hermes, is Son; and Mind is Father of the Word. They aren't separate from one another – for life is the union of Word and Mind. You and your inner talking, or Word, are one. If your mind is one with your inner conversations, then to be transformed in mind is to be transformed in conversation.

It was a flash of the deepest insight that taught Paul to write, *"Put off the former conversation, the Old Man which is corrupt, and be renewed in the spirit of your mind. Put on the New Man."*

"Put on the New Man," and *"be renewed in the spirit of your mind,"* is to change your inner conversation, for speech and mind are one. A change of speech is a change of mind.

The prophet Samuel said, *"The Lord spake by me, and his word was in my tongue."* If the Lord's Word was in the prophet's tongue, then the Lord's mouth that uttered the Word must be the prophet's mind, for inner conversations originate in the mind and produce tiny speech movements in the tongue. The prophet is telling us that the mouth of God is the mind of man, that our inner conversations are the Word of God creating life about us as we create it within ourselves.

In the Bible you're told that, *"The word is very near to you, in your mouth and in your heart, that you may do it. See, I have set before you this day life and good, death and evil, blessings and cursings. Choose life."*

The conditions and circumstances of life aren't created by some power external to you. They're the conditions that result from the exercise of your freedom of choice, your freedom to choose the ideas to which you will respond.

Now is the accepted time. This is the day of salvation. *"Whatsoever things are of good report, think on these things."*

For your future will be formed by the Word of God, which is your present inner talking. You create your future by your inner conversations. The worlds were framed by the Word of God, that is your inner talking.

That which ye sow ye reap. See yonder fields!
The sesamum was sesamum, the corn
Was corn. The Silence and the Darkness knew!
So is a man's fate born.
 - Sir Edwin Arnold, "The Light of Asia"

For ends run true to origins. If you would reap success, you must plant success. The idea in your mind, which starts the whole process going, is the idea that you accept as truth. This is a very important point to grasp, for truth depends upon the intensity of imagination, not upon "facts." When the woman imagined that her employer was unfair, his behavior confirmed her imagination. When she changed her assumption of him, his behavior reflected the change – *proving that an assumption, though false, if persisted in will harden into fact.*

The mind always behaves according to the assumption with which it starts. Therefore, to experience success, we must assume that we're successful. We must live wholly on the level of the imagination itself, and it must be consciously and deliberately undertaken. It doesn't matter if at the present moment external facts deny the truth of your assumption, if you persist in your assumption it will become a fact.

Signs follow, they do not precede.

To assume a new concept of yourself is to change your inner talking. You change the Word of God, therefore, put on the New Man. Our inner talking, though unheard by others, is more productive of future conditions than all the audible promises and threats of other people.

Your ideal is waiting to be incarnated, but unless you offer it human parentage it's incapable of birth. You must define the person you wish to be and then assume the feeling of your wish fulfilled in faith. Then that assumption will find expression through you.

The true test of religion is in its use, but culture has made it a thing to defend. It's to you that the words are spoken: *"Blessed is she that believed, for there shall be an accomplishment of those things which were spoken unto her from the Lord."*

Test it. Try it. Conceive yourself to be one that you want to be, and remain faithful to that conception, for life here is only a training ground for image making. Try it and see if life won't shape itself on the model of your imagination.

Everything in the world bears witness to the use or misuse of one's inner talking. Negative inner talking, particularly evil and envious inner talking, is the breeding ground of the future battlefields and penitentiaries of the world. Through habit people have developed a secret affection for these negative inner conversations. Through them they justify failure, criticize their neighbors, gloat over the distress of others, and in general pour out their venom on all. Such misuse of the Word perpetuates the violence of the world.

The transformation of self requires that we meditate on a given phrase – a phrase that implies that our ideal is realized – and inwardly affirm it over and over and over again until we're inwardly affected by its implication, until we're possessed by it. Hold fast to your noble inner convictions or "conversations."

Nothing can take them from you but yourself. Nothing can stop them from becoming objective facts. All things are generated out of your imagination by the Word of God, which is your own inner conversation. And every imagination reaps its own Words which it has inwardly spoken.

The great secret of success is a controlled inner conversation from premises of fulfilled desire. The only price you pay for success is the giving up of your former conversation – which belongs to the Old Man, the unsuccessful man. The time is ripe for many of us to take conscious charge in creating heaven on earth. To consciously and voluntarily use our imagination – to inwardly hear and only say that which is in harmony with our ideal – is actively bringing heaven to earth.

Every time we exercise our imagination lovingly on behalf of another, we're literally mediating God to that one. Always use your imagination masterfully, as a participant, not an onlooker. In using your imagination – to transform energy from the mental, emotional level to a physical level – extend your senses. Look and imagine that you are seeing what you want to see, that you're hearing what you want to hear, and touching what you want to touch. Become intensely aware of doing so. Give your imaginary state all the tones and feeling of reality. Keep on doing so until you arouse within yourself the mood of accomplishment, and the feeling of relief.

This is the active, voluntary use of the imagination – as distinguished from the passive, involuntary acceptance of appearances. It's by this active, voluntary use of the imagination that the Second Man, the Lord from heaven, is awakened in us.

People call imagination a plaything, the "dream faculty." But actually it's the very gateway of reality. Imagination is the way to the state we desire, it's the truth of the state desired, and the life of that state desired. If you could realize this fully then you'd know that what you do in your imagination is the only important thing. Within the circle of our imagination the whole drama of life is being enacted over and over again.

Through the bold and active use of the imagination we can stretch out our hand and touch a friend ten thousand miles away, and bring health and wealth to the parched lips of his being. It's the way to everything in the world. How else could we function beyond our fleshly limitations?

But imagination demands of us a fuller living of our dreams in the present. Through the portals of the present the whole of time must pass. Imagine elsewhere as here, and then as now. Try it and see. You can always tell if you have succeeded in making the future dream a present fact by observing your inner talking. If you're inwardly saying what you would audibly say, were you physically present and physically moving about in that place, then you've succeeded. And you could

prophesy from these inner conversations, and from the moods that they
awaken within you, what your future
will be.

For one power alone makes a
prophet: "imagination," the divine
vision.

All that we meet is our Word made
visible. And what we don't now
comprehend is related by affinity to the
unrecognized forces of our own inner
conversations and the moods that they
arouse within us. If we don't like what's
happening to us, it's a sure sign that
we're in need of a change of mental diet.
For man, we're told, *lives not by bread
alone, but by every word that proceeds from
the mouth of God."*

And having discovered the mouth of
God to be the mind of man – a mind that
lives on Words, or inner talking – we
should feed into our minds only loving,
noble thoughts. For with Words, or inner talking, we build our world.

O love, whose lordly hand
Has bridled my desires,
And raised my hunger and my thirst
To dignity and pride,
Let not the strong in me and the constant
Eat the bread or drink the wine
That tempt my weaker self.

Let me rather starve,
And let my heart parch with thirst,
And let me die and perish,
Ere I stretch my hand
To a cup you did not fill,
Or a bowl you did not bless.

- Kahlil Gibran, "Love"

"What have I said? What have I done?
O All Powerful Human Words!"

- William Blake, "Jerusalem"

Neville's advice should make it clear that the type of mindfulness we're talking about isn't passive, but active. We can objectively, passively watch the same thoughts for years, and they won't really change. Or we can voluntarily change them *right now* – through a gentle, focused attention on *feeling* what we wish to feel.

Usually, if something is bothering us, the latter choice is the better option. There are a few tips probably worth keeping in mind when you start practicing this type of mindfulness, but they can all basically be boiled down to this: *relax*.

The most important thing is to be relaxed.

You want to know how to easily change your "mental diet," and become more mindful? Do you want to know how to easily change your inner talking, and for it to be more to your liking?

Just relax.

Mindfulness works best from a state of inner relaxation.

That's the big key. And most adults completely neglect feeling relaxed as being an important part of their regular lifestyle. People are different, and everybody has different ways of feeling relaxed. It doesn't matter *how* you feel relaxed, but the deceptively simple solution to most of your problems in life *is just to feel relaxed more often.*

Some people like doing active things to help facilitate this feeling of relaxation, like exercising or dancing. Other people prefer quieter activities, like taking a walk or soaking in a warm bath. I personally like blasting music in the car and calmly driving down the highway. In short, it doesn't matter *what* you do to facilitate these relaxed inner feelings within yourself, the key is just *feeling* relaxed on a more consistent basis, and making these *positive feelings* a top priority every day.

Honestly, feeling more consistently relaxed is the *only* step required to completely transform your life. If you start feeling relaxed most of the time, your life will dramatically change for the better. Neville touched upon why that is: when we feel relaxed, our inner talking is coming from a peaceful, happy and abundant place. We're not bothered by our self-talk; we feel fine and content with what we're thinking about. And our outer physical world will soon start matching our relaxed inner talking.

So I suggest doing *whatever* you need to do to allow yourself to feel relaxed more often. This will take some trial and error on your part, which is totally fine and expected. It usually doesn't just happen overnight. You can't force relaxation, it happens on its own when you naturally feel in rhythm with what you're doing. You don't aim for perfection; you just start finding that wonderful inner rhythm more frequently. Start doing more activities that are conducive to making you feel this way; there are probably quite a few things you like doing that make you feel relaxed. Always encourage yourself to feel relaxed, only good comes of it, and with practice you'll find yourself feeling relaxed more often.

The reason relaxation is so effective in positively changing our life is deceptively simple. No one is judging us but ourselves, and if we stop being so harshly judgmental towards ourselves – and more relaxed instead – our world suddenly transforms itself. Very few people are aware of this. Even most "spiritual" teachers have no idea what we're talking about. My advice is to stop listening to their recommendations and just relax instead. Relaxation affords us the mental space needed to allow us to stop being so self-critical. And we can stop being self-critical of ourselves *immediately*.

There's really no need to believe you have to wait to feel relaxed. Start letting all those self-critical thoughts that float through your head just as naturally float away – they mean nothing. We don't needlessly have to entertain them for hours, days, weeks, months or years at a time. Welcome the negative thoughts in, and see them out just as quickly. They don't stay long as guests if we don't constantly entertain them.

You don't need to trust or give validity to negative thoughts. After a while, through trial and error, this will become quite clear to you. Negative thoughts – actually, *any* thoughts you have – are of no consequence, if you don't dwell on them. We become what we constantly think about, and that's because what we constantly think about we end up *assuming and feeling*. Everything else – the fleeting things we quickly think about, and then just as soon forget – quickly fades away. Cultivated feelings linger and shape our life; all other thoughts basically appear and then harmlessly disappear unless we decide to keep them company.

So by beginning to focus far less on negative thoughts – by going on a "diet" away from constant negative inner chatter – you start treating negative thoughts in a pretty indifferent fashion. *Your thoughts don't matter. Your feelings do.*

Negative thoughts begin to appear less frequently when you begin consistently *feeling* more positive. And when negative thoughts do pop up, they don't usually linger for as long. That's because you simply *don't care* that much about them. We don't try to forcefully combat them. If they're there, they're there. If they're not there, they're not there. So what? What difference does it make?

Becoming *indifferent* towards your thoughts is a very powerful thing. We don't try to improve our thoughts, that'd be too hard. We just gradually become more indifferent towards them. That's all we have to do. Your mental world changes for the better when you cultivate this indifference. That's because we naturally feel good when we're not overwhelmed by our thinking.

We surprisingly find a subtle goodness within ourselves when we're not overcome with negative thoughts. Life becomes smoother. And we can stop being overwhelmed by our thinking just by *being relaxed*. Spoil yourself in this regard, do it as much as possible – fully enjoy feeling relaxed.

When we feel relaxed, our imagination can also become more malleable to our liking, as Neville touched upon. Your deep inner feelings shape your outer destiny. What you assume and feel as real and true, you become. If you truly *assume and feel* yourself to be wealthier than you currently are, then you soon will become wealthier in the physical world. If you presently are sick, but start imagining and feeling yourself as being healthy, you will soon become healthier.

What we imaginatively assume and feel to be true will become true in our world – even when there are no rational indications that such things could possibly happen.

The key is to remain consistently relaxed most of the time. This isn't a goal-oriented practice in the traditional sense – *your only goal is to be relaxed*. Then everything will naturally arise from that. Results will happen purely because you're relaxed, and imagining specific desires is a completely optional practice. Nothing should be forced. For instance, if you would like to imagine having more money, *simply do so because it feels good to imagine such a thing*. The feeling is what counts, and what's pure. You shouldn't care about the results beyond that. In this instance, for example, you would just take pleasure in enjoying the wonderful feeling of having more money.

If you vividly imagine having something that you desire, *if you really feel it*, then there's nothing else needed in that moment. You have what you want. And, ironically, if you don't care about the outer results of these imaginative exercises beyond feeling them in that moment, then the outer results will inevitably arrive in your physical world sooner or later. *That's because everything positive originates from your positive, inner relaxed feelings of fulfillment.* Imagining specific things isn't the key – feeling relaxed is.

When we start working with our feelings, and tenderly begin to modify them, we often discover how stubborn we can be mentally. We realize how stuck we can become in negative self-talk, and in certain negative ways of thinking and feeling.

That's no problem, and nothing to be concerned about.

Over time these meddlesome mental habits start to disappear naturally. It happens almost effortlessly through increased relaxation. Be patient, and you'll be rewarded. This isn't something to try for a few days and then forget; this is something you can use for the rest of your life. All we have to do is allow ourselves to relax. We then become increasingly aware of our habitual self-talk – for good and bad – and through gentle practice can make our self-talk become more to our liking.

Feeling relaxed is the most important step you can take in order to easily change your life, and anybody can do it.

There's nothing selfish about being nicer to yourself – your self-compassion will naturally be mirrored in your outer world. You want to be helpful to others? *Help yourself first.* Only good comes of it. This is real mindfulness. Most people are totally unaware of how critical and non-loving they are to themselves throughout the day. The things we say to ourselves – the self-criticisms and judgments we make – are self-inflicted emotional daggers that keep us stuck in the mud. Through relaxation we naturally reconnect with our abundance. It's a practical tool, and it's yours to use, whenever you choose. Start paying more attention to your self-talk, become gentler towards yourself, and you're guaranteed to like what happens.

"Assume you are what you want to be. Walk in that assumption and it will harden into fact."

Mindful Manifestation
Keynote or Workshop

Imagine dramatically improving your well-being and transforming your organization...

Mindful Manifestation
with Tim Grimes

Tim Grimes speaks authoritatively on topics centered around stress relief, mindfulness and personal fulfillment. Drawing upon the brilliant teachings of Neville Goddard, Tim shares surprising ways for everyone to become more mindful and fulfilled by embracing relaxation as a paradigm for success.

To invite Tim to speak
at your next event email:
radicalcounselor@gmail.com

Part of the
NEVILLE EXPLAINS THE BIBLE
Series

Other books in the series include:

RELAX MORE, TRY LESS

MANIFESTING MIRACLES

MANIFESTATION THROUGH RELAXATION

THE POWER OF AWARENESS

FEELING IS THE SECRET

FREEDOM FOR ALL

WALKING WITH JESUS

PRAYER

MEDITATION

Taught by Neville Goddard
Edited by Tim Grimes

For more information visit:

www.radicalcounselor.com

Made in United States
Orlando, FL
12 October 2022